HOW TO SELL YOUR FARM SUCESSFULLY

OR TRANSFER IT TO THE NEXT GENERATION

ADRIAN SPITTERS FCSI, CFP, FMA

HOW TO SELL YOUR FARM SUCESSFULLY

OR TRANSFER IT TO THE NEXT GENERATION

Assante®
WEALTH MANAGEMENT

Be well-advised.

Copyright 2016 by Adrian Spitters, FCSI, CFP, FMA

ISBN: 978-1-895112-28-3

Published by
HeartBeat Productions Inc.
Box 633
Abbotsford, BC
Canada V2T 6Z8
email: heartbeatproductions@gmail.com
604.852.3761

Edited by:
Dr. Win Wachsmann
Cover design, artwork and digitally created images:
Dr. Win Wachsmann
Cover Photo: **rudall30 © 123RF.com**

Printed in USA

HeartBeat PRODUCTIONS

To farmers
who don't want to work forever

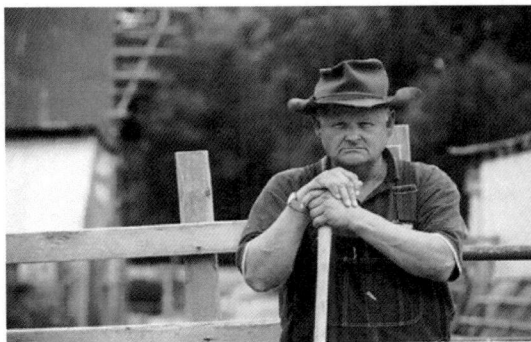

One day your farm will change hands...

Will you transfer your farm to your children, extended family, or sell to a third party?

Will it be on your terms?

TABLE OF CONTENTS

Introducing...

How to Sell Your Farm Successfully

or

Transfer it to the Next Generation

CHALLENGES, SOLUTIONS, AND WHERE TO
GET HELP

By

Adrian Spitters, Senior Wealth Advisor

Assante Capital Management Ltd.

CHAPTER 1

INTRODUCTION

modfos © 123RF

Most farmers don't have time to think too far ahead into the future. That's because they're busy attending to the needs of today: producing high-quality products, overseeing employees, and managing the mind-boggling number of details that go into owning a farm.

If they *do* think about the future, it's usually in terms of new government regulations, availability and price of land or quota for future expansion, or even what the weather will be like.

The truly long-term decisions, like when to sell or transition your farm (not to mention how to do it), are mentally filed away under the heading, "Bridges to cross when I've come to it."

But that bridge may be a lot closer than you think.

NO TIME TO DEAL WITH THE ISSUE

Understandably, most farmers have great difficulty in setting aside the time to plan for the future of their farm business in addition to working on their farm.

To quote John F. Kennedy, ***"The time to mend the roof is when the sun is shining."***

It is the planning for the future of your farm business while the sun is shining that will help protect your farm, and ultimately your family, from the rainstorms that loom ahead.

You see, recently conducted surveys[1] of privately-owned family businesses, including farms across North America, report that approximately 40% of business owners expect to exit their family business in the next five years. That number goes up to a whopping 70% within the next ten years.

[1] *The information from these surveys was derived from various sources, including Deloitte, PWC, Laird, Tyne, CFIB and MassMutual.*

These statistics are a direct result of the fact that baby-boomers are nearing retirement.

A significant number of these business owners indicate that they will be relying on the ongoing success of their business to finance their future lifestyle – either by selling the business, or from collecting a salary or dividend after they exit day-to-day management.

All this applies to farmers like you.

SO ASK YOURSELF

1. Do you have a plan in place to increase the value of your farm before it's time to sell?
2. Do you have a plan in place that will enable you to transfer your farm to your family or sell to a third party?
3. Have you planned how to retire on your terms, instead of being forced to transfer or sell your farm on someone else's?
4. Are you proactively preparing a successor who will enable the continuity of your farm operation?

Or are you one of the 65% of farmers who haven't planned that far ahead?[2]

[2] http://www.bdo.ca/en/Services/Advisory/Business-Transition/pages/The-BDO-SuccessCare-Program.aspx

It's true: most farmers haven't planned for the day when they will transition or sell their farm. That makes them vulnerable to an **involuntary sale**, meaning they will be forced to sell their farm due to death, disability, or other reasons.

As you can see, the question of when and how to transition your farm is something that needs to be answered sooner rather than later.

The first step is to have a plan. Having a plan in place *now* can save you untold time and trouble in the future…and it can also help ensure that when the time *does* come to transition your farm, you do it *right*.

The stakes are high. For an overwhelming number of farmers, the sale of their farm will be their primary source of income for retirement.

That's why it's crucial that they get it right. Otherwise, they will be denying themselves the chance at much-needed income during a time when every dollar counts.

For others, their major goal is to keep their farm in the family. But transitioning your farm, even to your own children, is a long and complex process.

Finally, *everyone* wants to cement their legacy and good name long after the transaction takes place.

I know that farmers are also ***business owners***...and that your business is one of the most important in the entire world. I understand that owning a farm isn't easy. Yet I also know that the decision to one day sell or transfer out of your farm can be just as difficult.

My name is Adrian Spitters. I'm a Senior Wealth Advisor with Assante Capital Management Ltd. As the child of a farmer, I can appreciate the hard work you've put into establishing a successful farm.

I've prepared this special book just for you. In just a few short pages, we'll look at some of the challenges facing farmers who want to quit working someday, what the most successful farmers are doing now, and where you can get additional help.

One of my goals is to give you ideas of how to plan for *your* eventual transition into retirement and the have peace of mind.

CHAPTER 2

THE CHALLENGES FACING FARMERS WHO WANT TO QUIT WORK SOMEDAY

modfos © 123RF

Here are two plain and simple truths. The **first** is that no matter how much you enjoy what you do, you probably don't want to do it forever.

At some point in our lives, we all want to wind down, explore other interests, and just generally live life at a slower pace. It's called retirement.

The **second** truth is that retirement is becoming increasingly difficult and expensive. This is especially true for farmers like you.

There are unique challenges you face that must be overcome in order for you to sell or transition your farm and retire the way you've always dreamed.

SOME CHALLENGES YOU WILL FACE

1. How to determine the value of your farm
2. Where and how to find the right buyer
3. How to choose the right time to sell
4. Deciding whether to transition your farm to a family member or sell to a non-related party
5. Determining whether selling your farm will bring in enough proceeds to fund your retirement and other financial goals.
6. Ensuring the orderly payment and transition of ownership/management of your farm to your successor/heir.
7. How to minimize the taxes that come from selling your farm
8. Ensuring you have sufficient assets to secure you and your family's future

AND THE BIGGEST CHALLENGE —
YOU DON'T WANT TO THINK ABOUT LEAVING

Underlying many of the reasons for failing to address the inevitable transition of their farm is the fear entrepreneurs have of leaving what they have worked so hard to build. The farm is their life and they do not want to give up control.

We can show you how you can gradually delegate control while finding a way to still employ your unique abilities. You can develop a track that will allow you to slowly step away from the farm while doing what is needed to protect your family and the farm.

WHAT ABOUT CONFLICTS WITH FAMILY
EMPLOYEES

It's amazing how often family dynamics become almost insurmountable when thinking about transitioning your farm.

One or more children may be working the farm while others have left the rural life behind. In family gatherings the discussion will rarely move in that direction.

However, everyone is giving it some thought. And that applies to your children and their spouses as well.

You love them all dearly but they will have different expectations of what the transition should look like.

As a result many farmers are reluctant to attempt reconciling the differing personalities, values and expectations that exist in their family unit.

They may try to defer the decisions and discussions, but there comes a time when all these issues will need to be addressed.

With the appropriate structures in place, you can address any potential conflict in advance and clear the way to moving ahead with a transition plan.

BUT IT'S STILL A FEW YEARS OFF

Now you may be thinking, "Retirement is still a few years off. Why do I have to think about this now?"

The answer is that by thinking and planning *now*, you can drastically improve your chances of retiring how you want to in the future. That's because, when it comes to selling your farm, you can either do it **by choice** or **by necessity**.

To sell by necessity means that you really have no other option than to sell your farm, often as quickly as possible. This is usually due to poor health, bankruptcy, or even a dramatic change in the industry.

The main problem with selling by necessity is that you often have to settle for a lower price. The other problem is that once your farm is sold, you will suddenly find yourself without a livelihood, and with no idea whether you have enough money on which to actually retire.

Selling by choice, on the other hand, means that *you* choose the timing and terms of your sale. *You* get to decide who you sell to and for how much.

Best of all, you can coordinate your sale within an overall retirement plan, factoring in your investments, taxes, and other financial goals.

The end result?

The knowledge that you can retire, stay retired, and make retirement everything you want it to be.

CHAPTER 3

THE NEED FOR A PLAN

modfos © 123RF

There's one thing that separates the farmers who sell voluntarily from those who sell by necessity: the former have a transition plan.

No matter how young or old you are, you need to have a plan. Saying "It's too early" is like saying, "I don't need to put my seatbelt on yet, I just pulled out of the garage. I'll wait until I'm on the highway."

The fact is, it's *never* too early. The sooner you have a plan, the sooner you can more ably avoid the unexpected bumps that every business owner faces at some point or another.

Dwight Eisenhower, former president of the United States, said it this way:

"Failing to plan is planning to fail."

THE BASICS OF A GOOD TRANSITION PLAN

Remember that a ***plan*** is a series of steps, determined in advance, designed to help you reach a specific objective.

The word "objective" is especially important. After all, you can't know what steps to take until you first know where you want to go.

So what might a transition plan look like?

I would like to suggest the following guideline for a farm transition plan. In the following chapters we will look at each one of these eight components.

1. Visualize your desired future	→	2. Analyze your current reality	→	3. Commit to creating a plan
6. Execute your plan	←	5. Design your farm transition plan	←	4. Create a solid wealth foundation
7. Achieve your desired future	→	8. Share your family's wealth		

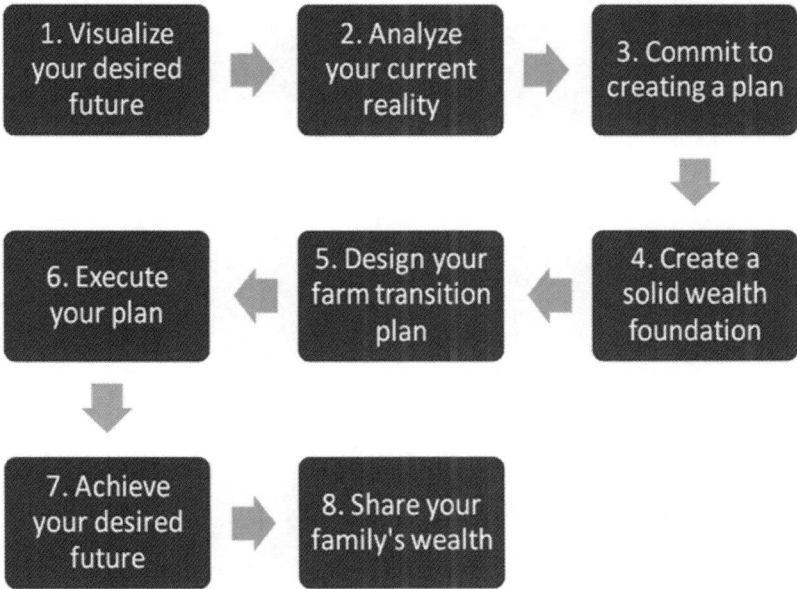

Please understand that this will not be an exhaustive discussion. For detailed steps and a wide range of planning documents, please contact the author. As a skilled advisor I have a wide range of resources available to assist you to make the best decisions possible.

This book is an introduction to the farm transition process - a task that may take several months and many conversations with family members and advisors.

CHAPTER 4

STEP 1
VISUALIZE YOUR DESIRED FUTURE

The first thing your transition plan should contain, then, is a **vision** of your desired future. Here is a sampling of the many questions that can be addressed. Feel free to add to the list.

1. What are your core values and principles?
2. Why do you continue to operate your farm?
3. What do you want to accomplish in your life?
4. What dreams do you have for yourself and your family?

5. What legacy would you like to leave?

6. Will you stay on the farm and continue in some fashion?

7. When (if ever) will you be ready for a change in lifestyle?

8. Have you discussed the above questions with your spouse?

9. Does your vision of retirement match up with your spouse's?

10. Have you discussed passing the farm to your farming child(ren) while balancing non-farming child(ren)'s interests?

Sometimes it is helpful to meet with a Wealth Advisor who would take the time to get to know your true fears, challenges, advantages, excitements, opportunities, lifetime goals and aspirations for you, your family, farm and legacy.

Their role is to help you visualize what your future could hold, and then create a summary report outlining the steps you should take to achieve it.

You will find a sample **Family Wealth Planning Checklist** – Chapter 21

CHAPTER 5

STEP 2
ANALYZE YOUR CURRENT REALITY

modfos © 123RF

2. Analyze your current reality

Next, an effective transition plan should include a thorough analysis of what I like to call your **current reality**.

This step involves exploring all areas of your personal, family and farm life that can have a financial impact on your wealth.

Think of it as an inventory of what you have to work with.

1. What is your current income?
2. What kind of expenses do you have?
3. What assets do you have? Real estate, stocks and bonds, RRSP's? Are you minimizing personal taxes on these non-farm assets?
4. What kind of liabilities do you have? Short term, long term?
5. How is your current health?
6. Are you maximizing income splitting opportunities with family members?
7. Are you farming as a proprietor, partnership or corporation? Do you know how to minimize tax exposure on your farming income in each scenario?
8. If you run the farm as a proprietor, do you understand how incorporation can save taxes in the years leading to retirement?
9. Do you understand how a Family Farm Partnership could create tax savings?
10. If you farm through a corporation here are some considerations:
10.1 Does your corporate structure ensure that your shares can "roll" to children in the event of your death rather than being taxed?

10.2 Do you know if your shares will qualify for the lifetime Capital Gains Exemption?

10.3 Have you obtained advice about whether you need a separate holding corporation?

10.4 Will your corporate structure allow for the most tax effective transfer of the operation to family members?

10.5 Do you understand how corporately held insurance can create a tax efficient succession plan?

As you can see, these are just a few of the questions that need to be addressed.

A discussion with a Family Wealth Advisor will bring many more questions to the forefront.

As you can see this process will require a lot of thought and planning.

You will find a sample **Family Wealth Planning Checklist** in Chapter 21.

CHAPTER 6

STEP 3
COMMIT TO CREATING A PLAN

3. Commit to
creating a plan

After examining some of the questions in previous chapters, you can see how important it is to make a plan.

Your next step should be to commit to creating a plan.

This means setting time aside to compile a list of all the questions (and answers if you have them) about every aspect of your farm business.

It's not about having time, but about making time.

In the same way you don't always have time to play with your grandchildren, you know you will make time to create memories and form bonds that will be remembered for many years to come.

Yes, the process may seem overwhelming.

However, just like every task you've ever taken on, it begins with that first step, that first shovelful, that first foundation.

How do you eat an elephant? One mouthful at a time. It may seem that this thinking and planning process is just like eating an elephant.

As you examine all the different parts of your farm business, you will soon realize that your lifetime of effort has created a living, breathing entity that will provide for you and your family for many years to come.

That accomplishment is something to be celebrated.

All those early, lonely hours, all that blood and sweat and all those tears have resulted in tangible and intangible assets of which you can be proud.

You have one more step, one more challenge ahead of you. To structure your farm business in such a way as to maximize the benefit for you and your family.

CHAPTER 7

STEP 4
CREATE A SOLID WEALTH FOUNDATION

photocreo © Photodune

4. Create a
solid wealth
foundation

This is all about you and your family's needs.

Your plan should also help determine what you ***need*** in order to reach your objective.

For example:

1. Do you need to enhance the value of your farm before you can sell it?

2. Does the future of your farm include your children, or extended family?

3. Do you need to minimize future taxes so that the sale or transition of your farm will not complicate things?

4. Do you need a higher return on your investments or less risk so that your wealth will be more secure?

5. Do you need a will and estate plan to ensure your family will be taken care of should anything unexpected happen?

6. Do you need to simplify your farm operations because you are spread too thin? Or do you need to expand and diversify to prevent all your eggs from staying in one basket?

These are just a few of the questions to ponder.

Like many farmers, your wealth is tied up in your farm. Once you have sold your farm, you need to create a solid investment foundation to manage the proceeds from the sale of your farm.

You will want to examine your needs are with respect to investing the proceeds from the sale of your farm or the cash you put aside prior to transferring your farm to your children to secure your retirement.

This will involve examining and quantifying your:

- risk tolerance
- liquidity requirements
- growth expectations
- insurance and annuity requirements
- income tax characteristics
- anticipated changes in lifestyle
- economic variables such as inflation and market volatility.

Because you have been busy running your farm, you will probably not have spent much time examining long term investment and wealth strategies.

What information you will have gleaned along the way will probably have come from accountants, lawyers and all those talking heads on TV who inhabit the financial channels and disseminate all that advice - some of which can be contradictory.

Where does one go for good, reliable advice?

Because we can't be experts in every field, we will need to speak with qualified, knowledgeable advisors.

Let me direct you to **Chapter 13 The Role of Advisors** where I will discuss in detail how to select a qualified and knowledgeable advisor.

CHAPTER 8

STEP 5
DESIGN YOUR FARM
TRANSITION PLAN

5. Design your
farm transition
plan

In the same way an architect helps you design and build a home or farm building, you need to have a plan designed by wealth planning professionals.

This plan will protect and enhance the value of your farm and minimize taxes in preparation for sale or transfer of your farm.

Up till now, you will have been using your own team of accountants and lawyers to structure and protect your business.

Farm transition however, can be a much more complex subject as you are learning from the previous chapters.

This requires a level of specialization that most lawyers and accountants don't have.

This is where a Wealth Advisor comes in.

A qualified, experienced and knowledgeable Wealth Advisor does not operate in a vacuum.

Over the years they will have built a team of wealth planning professionals on whom they can draw to help you design your plan.

The larger your farm business, the more complex the team will be.

They will work together with your lawyer and accountant(s) to analyze all possible solutions and design the best plan to preserve and enhance your wealth, and conceive a simple path for you to follow to achieve your desired future.

CHAPTER 9

STEP 6
EXECUTE YOUR PLAN

6. Execute
your plan

Once you developed *The Plan*, then it will be time to implement *The Plan*.

This will involve meetings – lots of meetings between you and your advisors.

Meetings to discuss *The Plan* and then meetings to begin implementing *The Plan*.

Meetings to document any major changes in your personal or financial situation that require an adjustment to *The Plan*.

This may take months, and maybe even years if you start soon enough or have a number of years to go before you want to go out to pasture.

You must be aware that *The Plan* is not fixed in stone but is a living and flexible document that may require changes and improvements.

Every year, all levels of governments play around with the rules and regulations that affect our lives.

With every federal budget, tax relief is provided or tax regulations are increased.

Keeping up with all those changes requires knowledge (your advisors) and decisions on your part to modify your plan to maximize the benefit to you and your family.

The most important characteristic you will need is **patience**.

Patience with the process and patience with all the people in the process who will need to be involved and kept up to date.

During this time, hidden family stresses and issues may arise. Some family members may change their minds about the details while others may no longer want to be involved.

CHAPTER 10

STEP 7
ACHIEVE YOUR DESIRED FUTURE

ptimages © Photodune

7. Achieve your desired future

Whew!

The implementation process is sometimes lengthy as the material is intense. It takes time to decide on the most efficient course of action for you to follow.

Once *The Plan* is complete, it will now be up to you to follow the steps in *YOUR PLAN.*

Remember all those dreams we discussed in Chapter 4?

By now you should see them coming to fruition.

Your long-suffering spouse is encouraging you to take a month or two and travel.

Isn't it time to let go and let the farm get along without you?

It's very hard, but you deserve the time off. Who knows you may even like it.

And the grandkids? They want to see you more often.

Admit it. You want to see them as well - for a while.

CHAPTER 11

STEP 8
SHARE YOUR FAMILY'S WEALTH

8. Share your
family's wealth

You've built your nest egg.

You've prepared for yourself and your family for the next generation(s).

You also want to help others.

With wise administration and strategic tax planning, you will be able to support your favourite charitable institution.

Whether it's the local food bank, a religious institution or funding high school and college scholarships and bursaries, your support will reap dividends for years to come.

CHAPTER 12

HOW DO I KNOW ALL THIS?

Adrian Spitters, FCSI, CFP, FMA
Senior Wealth Advisor

Farm life has always been an important part of my world. I grew up on a dairy farm on Nicomen Island near Mission, BC and have immediate family and relatives operating dairy, poultry and crop farms.

As co-executor (with two brothers) of my father's estate, I know all too well the result of not having a proper farm transition plan in place.

Our dad had a poorly executed, unworkable Will and a non-existent farm succession plan.

This led to family discord. Despite receiving the majority of the assets, the brother who inherited the farm suffered financial distress and became insolvent. A proper transition plan would have helped him get the financial and farm management training he needed.

Today, I work as a Senior Wealth Advisor with Assante Capital Management Ltd., a leading Canadian wealth management firm with extensive experience in family farm transitions. In my work with the *Assante Ag Group*, I provide wealth advisory services to farm and business families. This includes helping them grow and protect their assets while preserving their family wealth and legacy.

In my 29 years in the business, this is what I've seen: that all Canadians, especially farmers, need and want personalized financial advice that helps them achieve their life goals.

It is very clear to me that whether you have a transition plan in place or not, one day you will transfer your farm to your children, extended family or sell to a third party. The question is, will it be on your terms **(voluntarily)**, or someone else's **(involuntarily)**?

To that end, I have acquired great expertise by working with the wealth planning specialists I encounter as a member of the **Assante Ag Group**.

I specialize in developing specific and personalized strategies for each of my farmer clients.

I work to enhance their knowledge, provide guidance, and create peace of mind for each of them to enjoy.

CHAPTER 13

THE ROLE OF ADVISORS

GETTING THE HELP YOU NEED BUILDING YOUR OWN TRANSITION TEAM

Throughout the book I've written about talking with advisors and experts.

Successfully planning for and ultimately selling your farm will almost certainly require some expert help. There are so many legal, accounting, tax, and insurance implications that it's all but impossible for you to do it all on your own.

Getting a qualified valuation of your farm is also vital. *Fair market value* (for example) can be a very sticky issue with tax authorities, and trying to hand over your farm to your immediate or extended family at a "good" price can have unintended (and serious) consequences.

Most farmers feel busy enough without having to contemplate the complex – and sometimes unpleasant – possibility of selling or transitioning their farm someday. But unless they're planning on living (or working!) forever, "then an ounce of prevention is worth a pound of cure." You are best-served by engaging wealth management professionals to help make the process simple, easy, and *effective*.

Of course, you *could* work with individual professionals in all these areas (legal, accounting, tax, etc.) You may even believe you already have a plan for each of these areas.

WARNING

But there's a potential pitfall to that approach you must be aware of. When working with many disparate individuals, you could end up subject to conflicting and sometimes incomplete advice.

THE RESULT

You end up making essentially "random" investment, insurance, tax, trust, farm succession planning, and estate planning decisions that are all in isolation of each other. This will lead to a collection of investments, insurance, business, and trust structures that are fragmented, confusing, and not particularly tax efficient. When this happens, you become vulnerable to missed opportunities, unnecessary expenses, and unforeseen tax liabilities. It's not an exaggeration to say that the consequences could be catastrophic.

That's why an *integrated* transition plan is necessary. It's the only way to ensure everything is done right and nothing is missed.

There's another reason to hire a professional transition team to assist you. You see, some farmers never *really* retire, especially if they have transitioned the farm to their children. They still keep an eye on how the farm is run because they want to make sure their retirement remains secure. This creates a lot of stress both on the farmer and on his/her children. The farmer can't let things go, and the children can't really make decisions for themselves.

Here's the good news. With an experienced transition team, you don't have to keep a never-ending eye on your farm, because you don't have to worry about keeping your retirement secure. By working with a team to create a transition plan, you'll be able to extract enough assets from your farm to set up a separate retirement portfolio *before* you ever quit working. And you'll have increased confidence that your retirement is secure.

HOW CAN YOU FIND THAT EXPERIENCED ADVISOR

What Is Wealth Management And Why Should You Care?

Wealth management is more than just investment advice. Wealth management encompasses all parts of a person's personal and farm business life. A person's wealth is not just what they have in their investment portfolio – it's everything they have accumulated: their home, their cottage, their farm, other business interests, investment property etc.

To manage all these assets requires the advice of multiple professionals from accountants, lawyers, investment advisors, realtors, bankers, mortgage brokers, insurance agents, financial planners, estate planners and many more.

Most of these advisors usually work in isolation of each other. This can result in conflicting and sometimes incomplete advice, leading to bad financial decisions that happen in isolation of a person's overall financial objectives and needs.

The reality is, while most people have an investment plan, an insurance plan, a tax plan, and maybe even a farm succession plan and/or estate plan, these plans were most likely done for them at different times by different advisors in isolation of each other.

The result is a collection of investments, insurance, business and trust structures that are fragmented and not tax-efficient, resulting in missed opportunities, and unnecessary expense, unforeseen tax liability, duplication of obligations and at worst, catastrophic consequences.

Rather than trying to make sense of the sometimes conflicting advice from these professionals, farm families can benefit from a holistic approach to managing their wealth with a single advisor who coordinates all the services they need to manage their wealth and plan for their own and/or their family's current and future needs.

Wealth Advisors start by developing a plan that will grow and protect their clients' wealth based on their clients' personal financial situation, goals, comfort level, risk tolerance and needs.

This would encompass an investment plan to manage their investments, a risk plan to manage the risks to their wealth and livelihood, a personal tax plan to manage the tax implications of managing their personal wealth, a farm tax and succession plan to plan the sale or transition of their farm to new owners when they retire in a tax-efficient manner, and an estate plan to transfer their assets to the next generation tax-efficiently that also meets their wishes on who gets what and how.

Once all these plans are created, the wealth advisor works with their clients' own network of professionals to implement the various components of their plan and then meets with them on a regular basis to review and monitor the progress of their plans.

These plans are revised and updated when needed. Wealth Advisors touch every aspect of their clients' wealth from growing, protecting, and transferring their wealth to the next generation.

Most financial advisors are not Wealth Advisors. They do not have the knowledge or access to integrated wealth management services.

So how do you find a Wealth Advisor that can offer all the services mentioned above?

Good question!

Let's talk about the **7 Key Questions Every Financial Advisor MUST Be Able to Answer** before you hire them to manage your wealth so that you can achieve financial freedom, security and peace of mind!

Now… you may be expecting a series of questions like: "Do you have any samples of the types of portfolios you recommend?"

"What are your fees?"

"Can you show me testimonials?"

"How are your fees charged?"

"What is your track record?"

And all those are good questions. Any financial advisor worth their salt will have ready responses in place.

As someone who has been there in the trenches with the best of them, let me lay on you some queries the average financial advisor ISN'T expecting… which will enable you to see who's ready to advise you on your money and family wealth.

Ok here we go…

I have prepared a list of questions that you can ask. To access these questions click on the link below:

The 7 Key Questions Every Financial Advisor Must Be Able To Answer

Go to www.7keyquestions.ca

In this next section, I will be discussing
some specific issues in some detail
to demonstrate the wealth and breadth
of knowledge required to effectively
structure the farm transition.

Feel free to contact me for specifics.
(604) 855-6846

CHAPTER 14

SELLING YOUR FARM

maxym ©123RF

Essentially, you have two basic options for exiting the farming business.

1. The **first** is to sell to another person or another farmer. It's an arms-length transaction, and as such will often require the most effort and discipline. But it's also the option that usually provides the highest financial reward. These days, however, most farmers don't end up choosing to sell their farms. Instead, they take the second option.

2. The **second** – and more common – option is to transfer or sell your farm to the next generation of your family.

Management expert Peter Drucker, perhaps a little tongue in cheek, calls this **"the final test of greatness"** for business leaders…and that includes farmers.

Family dynamics make this choice arguably the most complex, and studies show this transfer to be successful in only around 30% of cases.[1]

Just 10% of businesses successfully reach the 3rd generation![2] However, the right amount of openness, clarity and respect between family members, along with legally sound transfer/sale documents, will go a long way towards making this option a great triumph.

[1] Family Business Institute
http://www.familybusinessinstitute.com/index.php/succession-planning/
[2] Family Business Institute
http://www.familybusinessinstitute.com/index.php/succession-planning/

CHAPTER 15

TAX STRATEGIES FOR FARMERS

alexeys © photodune

In this chapter I will make some broad observations.

As with the other subjects discussed, your mileage may vary.

This too will be an introduction and should not be construed as giving tax advice. That is best left to tax lawyers and tax investment specialists.

Tax strategies deserve special consideration for two very broad reasons.

The **first** is the tax-saving advantages that can be gained by planning properly long before you sell your farm.

The **second** reason is the not-so-pleasant tax repercussions that will occur should you sell or transition your farm improperly, particularly under the watchful eyes of the CRA (Canada Revenue Agency).

Fortunately, farmers have several options when it comes to minimizing the tax consequences of selling or transitioning their farm. Here are two important ones to know:

Option 1) Tax-free rollover

Remember how you can either sell or transition your farm? Imagine you decided to take the 2nd option, which is to transfer your farm to someone in your family.

The Income Tax Act of Canada allows for qualified farms to be transferred to children on a tax-free basis. In other words, you would not have to pay a tax on the transfer itself. Certain conditions have to be met for your farm to qualify, but this is certainly an option worth looking into.

Tax-free rollovers are very common among farmers. That's because farmers have special tax rules to adhere to which are different than the rules for general business owners. As a result, these types of rollovers apply only to farmers and fishermen.

Option 2) Capital Gains Exemption

This is perhaps the most popular tax planning technique.

With a Capital Gains Exemption, or CGE, you can sell qualified shares of a farm corporation and earn an exemption from having to pay a capital gains tax on the gains of up to $1,000,000 per spouse or individual family member with an ownership position in the farm and farm assets.

Note that for your children to qualify, advanced planning is required.

The $1,000,000 Capital Gains Exemption is also available to farm individuals on the sale of qualified farm property.

Qualified farm property includes:

- Farm land and buildings
- Shares in a family farm corporation
- An interest in a family farm partnership
- Quota

As with the tax-free rollover mentioned above, certain conditions apply. For example, if your farm corporation has excess cash or assets that are not actively being used in the daily operation of the farm, this may disqualify you from being eligible.

Also, if some of your farm assets do not qualify, steps will need to be taken to ensure that the farm qualifies. This can take years to do, meaning you should plan now to ensure all of your assets qualify.

Every farm and farmer is unique, and so is each farmer's tax situation. Remember, farmers have special tax rules that differ from those of non-farm businesses.

CHAPTER 16

ENOUGH FOR YOU AND YOUR FAMILY'S FUTURE

An important part of the transition process is to create a comprehensive plan encompassing all aspects of your financial life. By understanding what specifically about money is important to you, and how much you will need to achieve your goals, dreams, and lifestyle needs, you will have a better idea of when work can become optional for you instead of mandatory. This also helps give you the peace of mind you need in order to ensure you are exercising sound judgment when the time comes to sell or transition your farm.

Whenever you *do* decide to retire, it's critical that you have sufficient assets to provide a secure future for yourself and your family. There are a lot of factors to consider when it comes to this step, but there are two in particular that should be near the top of every list:

INCOME AND EXPENSES

Why are these two so important?

To put it bluntly, it all comes down to this simple rule. *You cannot retire successfully unless your income is more than your expenses.*

It sounds like a no-brainer, and it is. Yet I can't count the number of people I meet every week who have no idea what their income will be after their retirement...never mind if it will be more than their expenses. These people want to retire, they hope to retire, but they don't know if they really can.

Of course, there's more to retiring successfully than just being able to pay the bills.

Retirement is all about finally having the time and opportunity to try new things, go new places, and learn new skills. Here again is why income is so important. All those things cost money. So how do you know what you can do after retirement if you don't know whether you'll have the money to do it?

This is what you need to do. First, sit down and calculate what your income and expenses are *now*. Here are some questions you need to answer.

What is your monthly income after taxes?

How much do you pay in monthly utilities?

How much debt do you have, and what are your monthly payments like? Remember, this can include mortgage payments, car payments, credit card payments, etc.

How much do you spend on automobile insurance, home insurance, gas, and other regular expenses? Don't forget to consider any out-of-pocket medical costs.

Step 1:

Once you've tallied those numbers, subtract your expenses from your income. Whatever number remains is what's immediately available to set aside for retirement.

Now determine what expenses might change after retirement. For example:

What expenses will you have more difficulty paying once you are no longer drawing regular income from your farm?

What expenses do you currently have that will *decrease* after retirement?

What is your current tax bracket? Will it change after you retire and start earning less income?

Now comes the home stretch. Finish these final steps:

Step 2:

Take your existing expenses then add the amount of expenses that will go *up* after retirement. Next, subtract the amount of expenses that will go *down*. Hold on to that number for a moment.

Step 3:

Calculate the amount of income you expect to receive from Canada Pension Plan (CPP), Old Age Security (OAS) and any retirement accounts you have, like a Registered Retirement Savings Plan (RRSP), investment accounts, or Tax Free Savings Account (TFSA). Then subtract the tax you'll owe on these accounts once you start using them.

But remember: the order in which you draw income from these accounts is very important, because it will have a significant impact on how much net income you will receive in retirement and how long your retirement income will last.

You also need to consider the effect of inflation on your income and expenses. You may think you have enough when you retire, however you must factor in the official average annual rate of inflation, which is 2%.

In addition, retirees often find that their personal rate of inflation is much higher. Also, be sure to factor in a realistic rate of return on your retirement investments, or you may find after 20 years of retirement that you do not have enough to achieve all your retirement goals. The good news is that we can show you how long your money will last with inflation calculated into your plan.

Take the final number from Step 3 and combine it with the amount you can save from Step 1. Then compare it to the number from Step 2. Steps 1 and 3 combined is your income after retirement. Step 2 is your expenses.

Which number is higher?

Keep in mind that every number you reach from this exercise is just a loose estimate. Too loose, in fact, to make financial decisions by, but at the very least, this should get you thinking. And if you'd like a much more concrete projection of your income and expenses after retirement, all you have to do is give me a call.

Helping people plan for retirement is my specialty. I'd be happy to sit down with you, ask some questions, and prepare a comprehensive estimate.

Just contact me at (604) 855-6846 and we can schedule a time to meet for a visual demo.

In the meantime, just remember this fundamental truth: *you cannot retire successfully unless your income is more than your expenses.*

Remember, too, that your income should be enough to cover your wants as well as your needs. So start thinking about it today. It's a complex topic, but you've got plenty of time if you start working on it now.

To sum up, creating a formal farm transition plan should provide you with a blueprint of *what* your goals in life will cost, *how* to be able to afford them, and *when* to execute various strategies designed to help you achieve them.

CHAPTER 17

PREPARING YOUR FAMILY

PREPARING YOUR FAMILY FOR A SMOOTH AND EFFICIENT TRANSITION

Have you ever heard of the "**Six W**" questions? They go like this: **Who, What, When, Where, Why,** and **How.** If you are planning on transitioning your farm to a member (or members) of your family, each of these questions will need to be answered…and it's important that your family be involved. Too often, farmers make all the decisions by themselves, springing them on family members at the last minute. This can lead to mistakes, stress, and resentment…and ultimately, to a failing farm.

Answering the "**Six W**" questions isn't easy, but fortunately, you don't have to do it alone. While I focus mainly on the *financial* aspects of transitioning your farm, there are professionals out there who specialize in the family and emotional aspects.

Please contact me if you have questions about the family and emotional aspects of farm transition.

Feel free to contact me for specifics.

(604) 855-6846

CHAPTER 18

HOW CAN I HELP YOU?

modfos © 123RF

OUR FAMILY FARM TRANSITION PROCESS

Helping farmers create the kind of farm transition plan described above is my goal. I do this through the 8-step process outlined earlier.

Farmers who dream of retiring someday, are encouraged to sit down with me to discuss their farm transition plan.

HERE S HOW IT WORKS

The moment you walk through my door, you'll be treated like a client. I'll have a cup of coffee, or tea, waiting if you want it. When we sit down together, my philosophy is to first *listen* rather than speak.

I want to know about your goals, your dreams, your needs. What do you want to do with your farm? What do you want to protect? It's my job to learn these details. Only then will I suggest a possible course of action.

In this way, we can help you **visualize** your desired future. Then, we'll take stock of what you have to work with and what obstacles need to be overcome to reach that future.

We'll examine and list all your **Strengths, Weaknesses, Opportunities**, and **Threats (SWOT)**. This is how we **analyze your current reality**.

From here, farmers can decide whether they truly want to **commit to creating a plan**. Because they now have a greater understanding of what they want *and* what they have to overcome, we find at this point that most farmers are more excited and motivated to create a plan than ever before.

In order for any transition to be effective, however, farmers first need to ensure they have a **solid wealth foundation** on which to retire.

This is why we recommend that farmers take advantage of our **Integrated Wealth Management** services through Assante Private Client, a division of CI Private Counsel LP.

INTEGRATED WEALTH MANAGEMENT

"Integrated Wealth Management" means combining *every* aspect of your financial life into an overall plan.

This involves four main aspects:

- Your investment selections
- Your asset allocation
- Your taxes
- Your estate

Some farmers may have a few investments here and there, or have had their taxes looked at by a professional, or filled out a will several years ago. But most farmers don't have a plan in place for *all* these things.

Farmers who enlist my services, enjoy having each of these aspects working *in concert* together rather than separately. For example, doesn't it make more sense to know how your investments will affect your taxes, and vice versa? Doesn't it make more sense to factor in how your *heirs'* taxes will be impacted when your estate is passed onto them?

The fact of the matter is that most of your wealth is tied up in your farm. Selling or transitioning your farm will have a major impact on your overall wealth.

That's why it's so important to integrate every aspect of your wealth into your plan. It's the only way to ensure said impact will be positive instead of negative. Furthermore, once you have sold or transitioned your farm, you will need to have an investment strategy in place to better manage the proceeds from the sale, or the lump sum you extracted from the farm to secure your retirement.

Many farmers like to keep a constant eye on the farm even after they have technically handed off the day-to-day management duties. This is because they want to make sure their retirement remains secure.

By having an Integrated Wealth Management Plan in place, you'll be able to spend more time *enjoying* retirement and less time worrying about it. That's because your plan will likely recommend setting aside sufficient assets into a separate retirement account *outside* of your farm before retirement.

This is your retirement nest egg. More importantly, your plan will specify how much "sufficient" actually is. This way, once your account is large enough, you'll be able to generate income *before* you retire from the farm.

You know what that means: greater peace of mind. With your own retirement secure, you can more readily forego the daily grind and let your heirs run the farm and make decisions for themselves.

Ultimately, having an Integrated Wealth Management Plan means enjoying the fruits of your hard-earned labor, while your children begin making decisions on their own.

To put it simply, participating in our Integrated Wealth Management program will enable you to have a **solid wealth foundation** on which to retire.

YOUR FARM TRANSITION PLAN

Once your wealth foundation is in place, we can then **design a specific, personal transition plan for you**. During this process, we will connect with any other professionals you are already working with – attorneys, accountants, etc. – to create the simplest, most direct path from where you are to where you want to be.

Remember, your plan should help you:

1. Determine the value of your farm
2. Find the right buyer
3. Choose the right time to sell

4. Decide whether to transition your farm to a family member or sell to a non-related party
5. Determine whether selling your farm will bring in enough proceeds to fund your retirement and other financial goals.
6. Ensure the orderly payment and transition of ownership/management of your farm to your successor/heir.
7. Minimize the taxes that come from selling your farm
8. Ensure you have sufficient assets to secure you and your family's future

Once your plan is created, it will be time to **execute your plan**. But the responsibility shouldn't fall on your shoulders alone – we'll be there to hold your hand through the entire process. We do that by meeting regularly with you to review your plan and assess your progress. We will also work closely with your legal and accounting teams to implement all the financial, legal, insurance, and tax strategies your plan contains.

Then comes the best part. Executing your plan will enable you to reach your destination. To **achieve your desired future**. Even then, however, our work is not done. We'll meet with you every three-to-six months, or more often if necessary, to check in on how you're doing.

We'll also document any major changes in your financial situation that require us to adjust your plan.

Finally, we will assist you with the eighth and final step of the Farm Transition Process, which is to **share your family's wealth**. By this point, you have built a solid wealth foundation, sold or transferred your farm, and achieved your desired future. In this final step, we continue to meet with you *and* your heirs on an as-needed basis to ensure that your family's future – and your legacy – endures for generations to come.

OUR CLIENTS

If you are interested in learning more about our Farm Transition Process and Integrated Wealth Management Services, I'd love to hear from you!

In our experience, the services we offer work best with certain types of farmers. That's why our clients are part of a select group of farm families with a certain net worth who have decided to invest a portion of their assets with Assante Private Client. Assante Private Client is a division of CI Private Counsel LP, which houses the Wealth Planning Group (a specialized team to whom many clients of Assante Ag Group advisors have access).

Of course, whether you choose to become a client or not, it's always a good idea to at least come in for a free consultation. Together, we can help you understand some of your options and which path is best for you. From there, you can decide whether or not to continue with our planning process by becoming an investment client.

To learn more about how Assante can help you grow, preserve, and protect your retirement assets, please call me at (604) 855-6846 or email me at aspitters@assante.com.

SUMMARY

It should be clear by now that in order to reach your retirement goals, it may become necessary to sell your farm someday.

In order to sell your farm in a timely, cost-effective, and *profitable* manner, you need to have a farm transition plan.

It's this plan that will give you the step by step instructions needed to ensure the orderly transition of your farm to your buyer and/or your heirs, minimize taxes, and ensure you have sufficient assets for both you and your family's future.

CHAPTER 19

HOW DO YOU START THE PROCESS?

DO NOT DO IT ALONE

The world of finance has gotten more complex than ever. It takes years of time and training to master all the intricacies of financial planning, to say nothing of the laws and regulations that seem to change every year.

As a farmer, your time and energy should be spent on one thing: your farm.

That's why it's so crucial to choose an experienced, qualified wealth management expert to help you. Such an expert can answer your questions and look closely at your business before suggesting the best course of action. An expert can do the legwork and manage your plan, giving you confidence and peace of mind.

To demonstrate what a farm transition plan would look like, and how it would fit within our overall **Integrated Wealth Management services**, I'm currently offering a free consultation to farmers in Fraser Valley.

If you are reading this book in another province and want to meet with an Assante Ag Group Advisor, I can arrange an introduction for you.

All we'll do is sit down, have a cup of coffee, and look at your goals and needs. I'll explain some of the things you'll need to consider and where to get started. There's no obligation on your part. If you need further assistance from me, I'd be thrilled to provide it. If not, no matter. I'm just happy to help in any way I can!

If you want to take me up on my offer, just give me a call or e-mail me at aspitters@assante.com. We'll set up a time to meet whenever is most convenient for you. Keep in mind that the sooner we meet, the sooner you can have a plan in place. And remember...

If your goal is to quit working someday, creating a plan is a must.

Thinking about your future is a must.

Taking action is a must, too.

Don't waste another day. Start now!

Call me today: (604) 855-6846

CHAPTER 20

ADRIAN SPITTERS AND THE ASSANTE AG GROUP

Assante Ag Group

YOUR FARM. YOUR FAMILY. YOUR FUTURE.

The Assante Ag Group is a national farm advisory group that assists Canadian farm families in the areas of *tax planning, retirement planning, and wealth transfer*. As a member of the Assante Ag Group, I am part of a team of highly experienced and trusted wealth planning specialists that include lawyers and accountants with knowledge and experience in the tax and estate planning issues that affect farmers.

Taxation represents the single largest expense and loss of capital in the lives of many farm families, particularly in the retirement phase. As a member of the Assante Ag Group I work directly with the farm family to help them understand the complex tax and financial issues that need to be addressed in order to minimize loss of farm wealth when important transitions or transactions occur.

TAX, FINANCIAL AND ESTATE PLANNING

As an Assante Ag Group advisor, my main focus and strengths are tax minimization, wealth planning and estate planning, including:

Planning for the tax efficient transfer of the family farm to the next generation;

Pre-retirement planning for the tax efficient sale of farm equipment, inventory and other assets;

Planning tax efficient business structures for the family farm and other ventures;

Personal tax and estate planning;

Financial and retirement planning.

My approach is to bring together not only tax, estate and financial planning, but also tax efficient managed wealth solutions and insurance strategies, all personalized to meet the unique needs and values of each client family.

COORDINATING PROFESSIONAL ADVICE

The busy lives of farm families can seem further complicated by the necessary involvement of professionals from various disciplines, such as accountants and lawyers. As a member of the Assante Ag Group, I provide a comprehensive plan that coordinates the services of these professionals. This plan helps coordinate the implementation with the client family's accountant and lawyer, and continues to monitor the client family's tax and financial affairs thereafter and through the retirement years.

Financial Matters for Farmers – An invitation from Adrian Spitters

INITIAL INTRODUCTION

As an Assante Ag Group advisor, I provide a free initial consultation to introduce our wealth management program and to review your investment portfolio and financial situation for opportunities and income tax strategies.

WHAT YOU CAN EXPECT

Comprehensive financial planning encompassing tax, insurance, estate, and succession planning based on your long-term goals while still providing for the short-term needs of you and your family

A personal investment plan based on your goals, tax situation, income requirements, and risk tolerance

Access to tax lawyers, accountants, and insurance, estate and investment specialists

Identification, explanation and coordination of tax and estate planning strategies to be implemented by your professional advisors

Ongoing monitoring of your investments and regular reviews of your financial, tax, and estate plans

A COMMITMENT TO FARM FAMILIES

I am committed to maintaining the high levels of proficiency and expertise required to provide professional advice.

CHAPTER 21

FARM WEALTH PLANNING CHECKLIST

Here is a sample Farm Wealth Planning Check List

Wealth planning is more than investment returns

It is a process to maximize what you have, provide for your future and effectively pass it on.

Wealth planning is not just for the "wealthy"

It is something that everyone should do. It is never too early or too late to plan.

Wealth planning provides a financial framework for your life and beyond.

It is personal.It is customised. And it works.

BIG PICTURE

My 3 biggest concerns today are:

1. _____

_____

_____

2. _____

_____

_____

3. _____

_____

_____

What are your most important planning objectives	NOT Important	Important	VERY Important
Identifying all the issues you need to consider: financial, retirement, tax, succession or sale issues			
Having enough money to sustain your desired lifestyle in retirement			
Structuring your affairs to minimize tax now, at retirement and on death			
Maximizing returns in your investment portfolio			
Deciding whether/when you will be ready for a change in lifestyle			
Passing the farm to your farming child(ren) while balancing non-farming child(ren)'s interests			
Taking care of others in the event of your illness, disability or death - parents, children, grandchildren			
Leaving a personal legacy - values, traditions, ethics, life lessons and inheritance			
Paying for children's or grandchildren's education			
Maximizing a gift/bequest to your favorite charity			
Avoiding probate fees			
Avoiding family conflict after you're gone			

Retirement Planning	NOT Important	Important	VERY Important
Do you have a plan for when, or if, you will retire from active farming & a clear vision of your life in retirement?			
Do you and your spouse agree on what your lifestyle will be in retirement?			
Do you know how much you can spend monthly/annually during retirement without outliving savings?			
Is it important to diversify into some non-farm assets?			
Is eliminating all income tax every year the best retirement planning?			
Can you minimize current taxes and also save for retirement at the same time?			
Can you hold retirement savings so they doen't interfere with farm tax planning opportunities?			
Do you know how many years in advance you must start planningg for retirement?			
Why is it hard to defer income in the years before retirement?			
Will you need to rely on government pension for income?			
Will your Old Age Security benefits be subject to clawbacks?			
Which retirement income sources should you spend first to minimize taxes?			

Tax Planning	NOT Important	Important	VERY Important
Are you sure are currently minimizing unnecessary exposure to tax?			
Are you minimizing personal taxes on non-farm assets such as investments?			
Are you maximizing all income splitting opportunities with spouse & children?			
Do you know which assets can be rolled over tax free to your spouse and which are taxed at death?			
Do you know about "rollover" of land, equipment and production quota and when it can be denied?			
Will farm rollover be available for each separate quarter/half/section you own?			
Do you know what your lifetime Capital Gains Exemption (CGE) is and which assets are eligible?			
Do you qualify for lifetime Capital Gains Exemption (CGE) for each separate quarter/half/section you own?			
If you farm as a proprietor, do you know how:			
- to minimize tax exposure?			
- a Family FArm Partnership saves taxes?			
- how incorporating can save taxes?			

Tax Planning	NOT Important	Important	VERY Important
If you farm through a corporation:			
- are you confident you are minimizing your corporate tax bill?			
- does your corporate structure ensure your shares can "roll" down to your children rather than being taxed when you die?			
- do you know if your shares will qualify fo a lifetime Capital Gains Exemption (CGE)			
- does your corporate structure ensure your shares will always qualify for the lifetime Capital Gains Exemption (CGE)			
- have you obtained advice about whether you need a separate holding corporation			
- does your farm business succession plan provide for the most tax effective transfer of shares to family members?			
- do you understand how corporately held insurance can create a tax efficient succession plan?			
- do you know if you are maximizing access to the lowest corporate tax rate?			

Estate Planning	NOT Important	Important	VERY Important
Do you know:			
- how taxes will affect your estate			
- how much your estate will pay in probate fees			
Do you know how tax will impact your:			
- non-registered investments?			
- registered assets (RRSP's, RRIF's)?			
- other assets such as real estate?			
Do you understand how the farm rollover rules apply at death?			
Have you completed a recent inventory of:			
- assets of significant value?			
- personal effects?			
- items of emotional value?			
Do you know the difference between "joint tenancy" and "tenancy in common" and the reasons for using the various ownership methods?			
Have you made, or do intend on making gifts during your lifetime?			
Do you have a current will?			
Have you specifically discussed your estate plan with your family?			

Estate Planning	NOT Important	Important	VERY Important
Have you specifically discussed your intentions regarding your farming operation with your children?			
Have you obtained advice about ways to create a "fair" distribution of estate value between farming and non-farming children?			
Do you have any concerns about:			
- how your beneficiaries will manage and spend their inheritance			
- how your family will deal with the family cottage?			
Do you know all the uses of trusts and how they can benefit you and your beneficiaries?			
- do you understand how trusts can save Income Trust?			
- do you understand how trusts can protect your children from marriage breakdown or creditor claims?			
Have you selected...			
- an Executor or alternate Executor			
- a guardian for minor children			
- a Power of Attorney for financial and property matters?			
- a Power of Attorney for personal and life decisions?			

List below any issues you want to discuss with:

1. Family Members:

_____

_____

_____

2. Partners or Shareholders in Your farming Operation:

_____

_____

_____

3. Your Financial Advisor:

_____

_____

_____

Adrian Spitters

Senior Wealth Advisor

Assante Capital Management Ltd.

604 - 855 - 6846 •

aspitters@assante.com

Published by

HeartBeat Productions

Box 633

Abbotsford, BC

Canada V2T 6Z8

email: heartbeatproductions

604.852.3761

Adrian Spitters *FCSI, CFP, FMA*

Senior Wealth Advisor

Farm life has always been an important part of my world. I grew up on a dairy farm on Nicomen Island near Mission, BC and have immediate family and relatives operating dairy, poultry and crop farms.

As co-executor (with two brothers) of my father's estate, I know all too well the result of not having a proper farm transition plan in place.

Our dad had a poorly executed, unworkable Will and a non-existent farm succession plan.

This led to family discord. Despite receiving the majority of the assets, the brother who inherited the farm suffered financial distress and became insolvent. A proper transition plan would have helped him get the financial and farm management training he needed.

Today, I work as a Senior Wealth Advisor with Assante Capital Management Ltd., a leading Canadian wealth management firm with extensive experience in family farm transitions. In my work with the *Assante Ag Group*, I provide wealth advisory services to farm and business families. This includes helping them grow and protect their assets while preserving their family wealth and legacy.

In my 29 years in the business, this is what I've seen: that all Canadians, especially farmers, need and want personalized financial advice that helps them achieve their life goals.

It is very clear to me that whether you have a transition plan in place or not, one day you will transfer your farm to your children, extended family or sell to a third party. The question is, will it be on your terms **(voluntarily)**, or someone else's **(involuntarily)**?

To that end, I have acquired great expertise by working with the wealth planning specialists I encounter as a member of the **Assante Ag Group**.

I specialize in developing specific and personalized strategies for each of my farmer clients.

I work to enhance their knowledge, provide guidance, and create peace of mind for each of them to enjoy.

Adrian Spitters •
Senior Wealth Advisor •
Assante Capital Management Ltd.
604 - 855 - 6846 •
aspitters@assante.com
Web: www.yourfarmtransitionadvisor.ca

This material is provided for general information and should not be considered personal, tax, or investment advice. The information contained herein is subject to change without notice.. Every effort has been made to compile this material from reliable sources however no warranty can be made as to its accuracy or completeness. Assante Wealth Management (Canada) Ltd. and its dealer subsidiaries accept no responsibility for any loss arising from the use of and reliance on the information contained herein. Before acting on any of this information, please make sure to see me for individual financial advice based on your personal circumstances. Please visit www.assante.com/legal.jsp or contact Assante at 1-800-268-3200 for information with respect to important legal and regulatory disclosures relating to this notice. Assante is an indirect, wholly-owned subsidiary of CI Financial Corp. ("CI"). The principal business of CI is the management, marketing, distribution and administration of mutual funds, segregated funds and other fee-earning investment products for Canadian investors through its wholly-owned subsidiary CI Investments Inc. If you invest in CI products, CI will, through its ownership of subsidiaries, earn ongoing asset management fees in accordance with applicable prospectus or other offering documents. Assante Capital Management Ltd. is a member of the Canadian Investor Protection Fund and is registered with the Investment Industry Regulatory Organization of Canada.

The Assante Ag Group is comprised of Assante Financial Management Ltd. (AFM) advisors and Assante Capital Management Ltd. advisors (ACM).

Wealth Planning Services may be provided by an accredited Assante Advisor or Assante Private Client, a division of CI Private Counsel LP.

Assante Private Client is a division of CI Private Counsel LP.

Insurance products and services are provided through Performance Financial Consultants Ltd

The (sample) Farm Wealth Planning checklist has been reproduced with permission Tracking #54679D